# Gorillas

David and Patricia Armentrout

Rourke
Publishing LLC
Vero Beach, Florida 32964

www.rourkepublishing.com

PHOTO CREDITS: Cover ©Timothy Craig Lubcke;
title page ©Emin Kuliyev; pg. 04 ©Timothy Craig Lubcke; pg. 05 ©Steffen Foerster; pg. 06 ©Petre de Ruiter; pg. 08 ©Yoka Van Eekelen; pg. 09 ©Donald Gargano; pg. 10 ©Kevdog; pg. 11 ©Russell McBride; pg. 12 ©Karen Givens; pg. 14, 16 ©PhotoDisc; p15 ©Mark Atkins; pg. 17 ©International Fund For Animal Welfare; pg. 18 ©Yves Grau; pg. 19 ©Wolfgang Moeller; pg. 20 ©Timothy Craig Lubcke; pg. 21 ©Steffen Foerster; pg. 22 ©Hans Meerbeek

Editor: Robert Stengard-Olliges

Cover design by: Nicola Stratford, bdpublishing.com

**Library of Congress Cataloging-in-Publication Data**

Armentrout, David, 1962-
Gorillas / David and Patricia Armentrout.
p. cm. -- (Amazing apes)
ISBN 978-1-60044-567-5
1. Gorilla--Juvenile literature. I. Armentrout, Patricia, 1960- II. Title.
QL737.P96A756 2008
599.884--dc22
2007011851

**Printed in the USA**

CG/CG

Rourke Publishing

www.rourkepublishing.com – rourke@rourkepublishing.com
Post Office Box 3328, Vero Beach, FL 32964

# Table of Contents

## Gentle Giants

You may know that gorillas are large, powerful apes. But did you know that gorillas are **primates**, just like humans and monkeys? Gorillas are the largest primates in the world. But despite their great size, gorillas are gentle giants.

Primates are mammals with hands, fingernails, and forward-facing eyes.

## Knuckle Walking

Gorillas are wonderful to look at. They have large heads with intelligent looking faces. Short, dark brown or black hair covers most of their body. Gorillas usually walk on all fours. To protect their sensitive fingertips, gorillas walk on their knuckles.

Adult female gorillas can weigh up to 200 pounds (90 kg). They are fully mature by eight years old. Females produce **offspring** every three to five years.

Adult male gorillas are impressive animals. They can weigh 400 pounds (181 kg) or more. Mature males are called silverbacks because of silvery hair on their back.

## Big Eaters

Gorillas are mainly vegetarians. Except for the occasional insect, gorillas don't eat meat. Gorillas eat leaves, bark, and fruit. They roam the forests searching for their favorite foods.

An adult male can
eat more than 50 pounds
(22 kg) of food every day.
That's a lot of leaves!

# Silverbacks

A group of gorillas is called a troop.

## Gorilla Families

Gorillas live in family groups. Some may have only two or three members, while others have 30 or more. A silverback leads a family group. He makes important decisions for the group and protects his family.

# Shrinking Habitat

Outside of zoos, gorillas live only in the tropical forests of central Africa. Humans are also interested in the land that gorillas call home. Unfortunately, humans destroy much of the gorilla's forest **habitat** by cutting down the forests and using the land for farming.

Mediterranean Sea
Persian Gulf
Red Sea
Gulf of Aden
AFRICA
Atlantic Ocean
Indian Ocean
Western Lowland Gorilla
Mountain Gorilla
Eastern Lowland Gorilla

Gorillas need large areas of undisturbed forest to thrive. As their forest habitat disappears, so do the gorillas. Gorillas are also hunted for food in some areas. Gorillas are an **endangered species**. This means that one day gorillas may become extinct.

## Eastern Gorillas

Eastern gorillas are a species of gorilla that live in the east central lowland forests of Africa. They are the largest gorillas. A subspecies of eastern gorillas, the mountain gorilla, inhabits the mountain regions. Mountain gorillas are highly endangered. Scientists estimate there are less than 700 mountain gorillas left in the wild.

# Western Gorillas

Western gorillas are more common than their eastern cousins. As many as 100,000 western gorillas inhabit the lowlands of west central Africa.

## An Uncertain Future

Gorillas are truly amazing apes. Gorillas remind us of ourselves. They look and sometimes act like humans. The strong connection between humans and apes may be the gorilla's best hope for survival.

# Glossary

**endangered species** (en DAYN jurd SPEE seez) — a species or type of animal that is in danger of disappearing forever

**habitat** (HAB uh tat) — the natural home of an animal or plant

**offspring** (OFF spring) — an animal's young

**primates** (PRY maytz) — a group of intelligent mammals that includes monkeys, apes, and humans

## Index



## FURTHER READING

De Medeiros, Michael. *Gorillas*. Weigl Publishers, 2006.
Goldish, Meish. *Gorillas.* Bearport Publishing, 2007.
Imbriaco, Alison. *The Mountain Gorilla*. Enslow Publishers, 2006.

## WEBSITES TO VISIT

www.worldwildlife.org/apes
nationalzoo.si.edu/Animals/Primates/
www.nationalgeographic.com/kids/creature_feature/0007/gorillas.html

## ABOUT THE AUTHOR

David and Patricia Armentrout have written many nonfiction books for young readers. They have had several books published for primary school reading. The Armentrouts live in Cincinnati, Ohio, with their two children.